Prayers in the Storm

TEXT AND PAINTINGS BY

Sandy Lynam Clough®

HARVEST HOUSE PUBLISHERS

EUGENE, OREGON

Prayers in the Storm

Text Copyright © 2002 by Sandy Lynam Clough
Published by Harvest House Publishers
Eugene, OR 97402

Library of Congress Cataloging-in-Publication Data

Clough, Sandy Lynam, 1948-
    Prayers in the Storm / Sandy Lynam Clough.
        p. cm.
    ISBN 978-0-7369-0828-3
    1. Consolation.   I. Title.
    BV4905.3 .C58 2002
    242' .4--dc21

                                        2002001749

Design and production by Garborg Design Works, Minneapolis, Minnesota

Verses marked NASB are taken from the New American Standard Bible ®, © 1960, 1962, 1963, 1968, 1971,
1972, 1973, 1975, 1977, 1995 by The Lockman Foundation. Used by permission. Verses marked AMP are
taken from The Amplified Bible, Old Testament, Copyright © 1965 and 1987 by The Zondervan
Corporation, and from The Amplified New Testament, Copyright © 1954, 1958, 1987 by The Lockman
Foundation. Used by permission. Verses marked TLB are taken from The Living Bible, Copyright © 1971.
Used by permission of Tyndale House Publishers, Inc., Wheaton, Illinois 60189. All rights reserved.

Printed in China

10 11 12 13 14 /NG/ 12 11 10 9 8

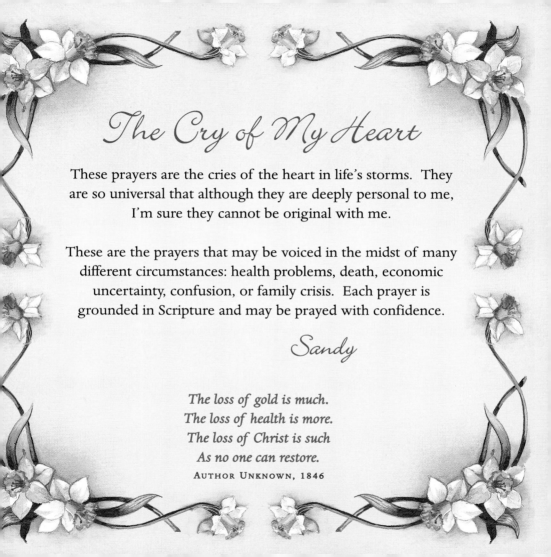

The Cry of My Heart

These prayers are the cries of the heart in life's storms. They are so universal that although they are deeply personal to me, I'm sure they cannot be original with me.

These are the prayers that may be voiced in the midst of many different circumstances: health problems, death, economic uncertainty, confusion, or family crisis. Each prayer is grounded in Scripture and may be prayed with confidence.

Sandy

The loss of gold is much.
The loss of health is more.
The loss of Christ is such
As no one can restore.
AUTHOR UNKNOWN, 1846

How do I pray when I already know what the results of my circumstances are going to be? How do I pray when I know nothing is going to change, apart from an absolute miracle, and I can't change anything? When death is coming and healing has not? When divorce is coming and reconciliation is not? When a job is lost and cannot be regained?

I can only stand and ask the Lord to be strong in all my weakness and helplessness.

But He said to me, My grace (My favor and loving-kindness and mercy) is enough for you [sufficient against any danger and enables you to bear the trouble manfully]; for My strength and power are made perfect (fulfilled and completed) and show themselves most effective in [your] weakness. Therefore, I will all the more gladly glory in my weaknesses and infirmities, that the strength and power of Christ (the Messiah) may rest (yes, may pitch a tent over and dwell) upon me!

2 CORINTHIANS 12:9 AMP

Dear Lord,

In this storm that will not end without loss, I ask that the strength and power of Christ may rest on me—that it may actually pitch a tent over me and dwell upon me.

Amen.

5

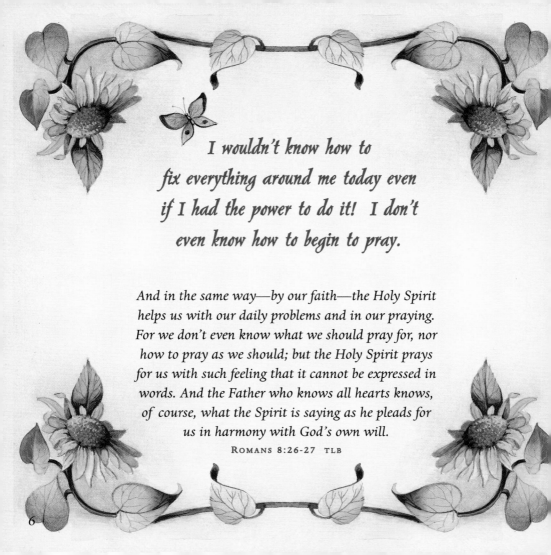

*I wouldn't know how to
fix everything around me today even
if I had the power to do it! I don't
even know how to begin to pray.*

*And in the same way—by our faith—the Holy Spirit
helps us with our daily problems and in our praying.
For we don't even know what we should pray for, nor
how to pray as we should; but the Holy Spirit prays
for us with such feeling that it cannot be expressed in
words. And the Father who knows all hearts knows,
of course, what the Spirit is saying as he pleads for
us in harmony with God's own will.*

ROMANS 8:26-27 TLB

Dear Lord,

I am compressed by stresses on every side. I don't even know what to ask for or exactly what I need for You to do. I need You to pray for me.

Amen.

Sometimes it seems that storms come in seasons. Have you ever, in weary frustration, thrown up your hands and cried, "Give me a break!"

I long, yes, faint with longing to be able to enter your courtyard and come near to the Living God. Even the sparrows and swallows are welcome to come and nest among your altars and there have their young, O Lord of heaven's armies, my King and my God! How happy are those who can live in your Temple, singing your praises.

PSALM 84:2-4 TLB

Dear Lord,

Today I am desperate for a place of rest. Please draw me into Your courts and into Your presence. Just like a little sparrow, I want to find a place and settle into a nest there—tucked away in Your presence until I can draw strength from You and face the storm again.

Amen.

As a consumer, more than once when I have had a problem with goods or services, I have asked customer service to let me speak with a supervisor. Hoping for someone with the authority and ability to help me, I can't help but think of the owner of the company. If only he or she knew, surely they would want to help me!

What an awesome thing it is to contemplate that the Creator and Lord of the universe invites me to bring my needs and concerns directly before Him. Jesus is the way to the Father. Because of Him, I am welcome to come before the Lord God.

At that time you will ask (pray) in My Name; and I am not saying that I will ask the Father on your behalf [for it will be unnecessary]. For the Father Himself [tenderly] loves you because you have loved Me and have believed that I came out from the Father.

<small>JOHN 16:26-27 AMP</small>

So let us come boldly to the very throne of God and stay there to receive his mercy and to find grace to help us in our times of need.

<small>HEBREWS 4:16 TLB</small>

Dear Lord,

Thank You for giving me access to You. What would I do without it? I would be without hope or help. With it, I have access to everything I need and everything You are. You have offered me an incredible privilege.

Amen.

When my children were little we lived in Florida and experienced some pretty lively thunderstorms. One night during a particularly noisy storm, to calm their fears I let loose with a rousing rendition of a favorite old hymn, "No, Never Alone."

The louder the storm rumbled and boomed, the louder I thundered and sang…

"I've seen the lightning flashing and heard the thunder roll…."

Adding the chorus with gusto:
"No, never alone. No, never alone.
He promised never to leave me,
Never to leave me alone."

The storms I have faced since haven't all been quite so noisy, but they have tried to conquer my soul. I have never given up because He has never left me alone.

I will never desert you, nor will I ever forsake you.

HEBREWS 13:5 NASB

Dear Lord,

Thank You that above the
noise of this storm is
Your promise—You
will not leave me alone.

Amen.

13

In the Old Testament, the Lord told Moses to send out scouts to explore the land of Canaan, the Promised Land that He had given to the Israelites. The scouts found a land lush with fruit and flowing with milk and honey. But ten of the scouts were afraid because the people who lived there were strong and large and their cities were fortified. Their bad report caused the people to grumble against Moses and the Lord for leading them there.

But Joshua and Caleb were the two scouts who brought back a different report:

Could it be that the storm I fear is an opportunity for growth?

The land through which we passed as scouts is an exceedingly good land. If the Lord delights in us, then He will bring us into this land and give it to us, a land flowing with milk and honey. Only do not rebel against the Lord, neither fear the people of the land for they are bread for us.

NUMBERS 14:7-9 AMP

Dear Lord,

I ask You to make
this storm "bread"
for me. I ask You to use
it to expand my life.

Amen.

15

*S*cripture tells us that after Jesus and His disciples set out to cross a large lake, a terrible storm arose. High waves were breaking over the boat until it was filled up with water and about to sink.

Jesus was asleep at the back of the boat.

Frantically they wakened him, shouting
"Teacher, don't you even care that we
are all about to drown?"

Then he rebuked the wind and said to the sea,
"Quiet down!" And the wind fell, and there
was a great calm!

And he asked them, "Why were you so fearful?
Don't you even yet have confidence in me?"

Mark 4:38-40 TLB

16

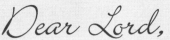

Dear Lord,

You slept in a storm. I always figured that You could do that because You knew that You could control the storm. I can't control this storm in my life, and I can't sleep through it.

Please give me the peace You have about my storm.

Amen.

18

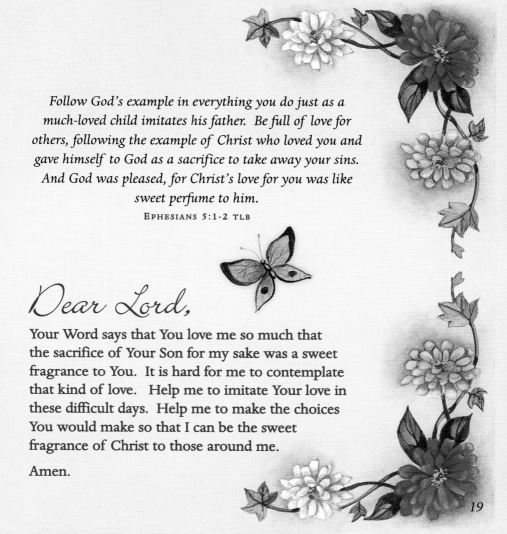

Follow God's example in everything you do just as a much-loved child imitates his father. Be full of love for others, following the example of Christ who loved you and gave himself to God as a sacrifice to take away your sins. And God was pleased, for Christ's love for you was like sweet perfume to him.

EPHESIANS 5:1-2 TLB

Dear Lord,

Your Word says that You love me so much that the sacrifice of Your Son for my sake was a sweet fragrance to You. It is hard for me to contemplate that kind of love. Help me to imitate Your love in these difficult days. Help me to make the choices You would make so that I can be the sweet fragrance of Christ to those around me.

Amen.

The greatest love is shown
when a person lays down his life for
his friends; and you are my friends if
you obey me...You didn't choose me!
I chose you! I appointed you to go and
produce lovely fruit always, so that no
matter what you ask for from the Father,
using my name, he will give it to you.

JOHN 15:13-16 TLB

Dear Lord,

Thank You for calling me
Your friend and giving me
permission to ask for
what I need.

Amen.

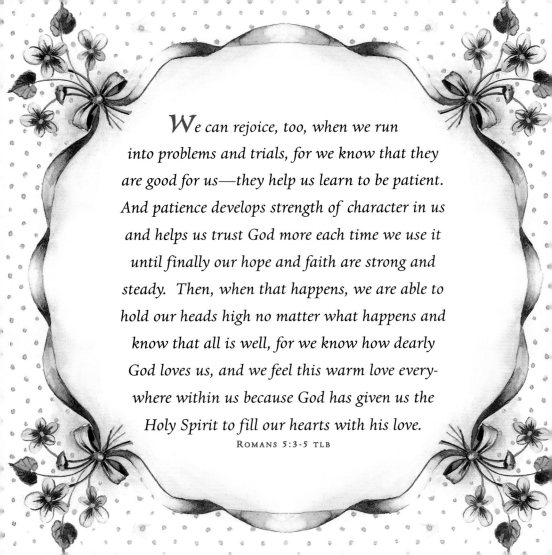

We can rejoice, too, when we run into problems and trials, for we know that they are good for us—they help us learn to be patient. And patience develops strength of character in us and helps us trust God more each time we use it until finally our hope and faith are strong and steady. Then, when that happens, we are able to hold our heads high no matter what happens and know that all is well, for we know how dearly God loves us, and we feel this warm love everywhere within us because God has given us the Holy Spirit to fill our hearts with his love.

ROMANS 5:3-5 TLB

Dear Lord,

I am determined to know You.
What is there about You that You
want to teach me in this storm?
Amen.

Casting the whole of your care...on Him, for He cares for you affectionately and cares about you watchfully.

1 PETER 5:7 AMP

Cast your burden on the Lord...and He will sustain you.

PSALM 55:22 AMP

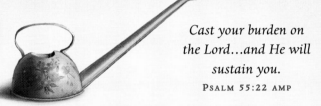

Dear Lord,

Elevators have load limits! Bridges have load limits! I have a load limit, and I have reached it. You have told me to cast my cares on You, but I'm having trouble lifting this load off myself. Please transfer it from me to You.

Amen.

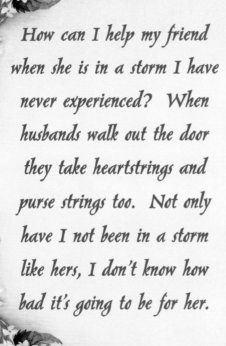

How can I help my friend when she is in a storm I have never experienced? When husbands walk out the door they take heartstrings and purse strings too. Not only have I not been in a storm like hers, I don't know how bad it's going to be for her.

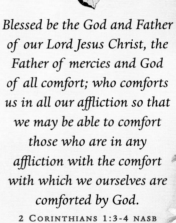

Blessed be the God and Father of our Lord Jesus Christ, the Father of mercies and God of all comfort; who comforts us in all our affliction so that we may be able to comfort those who are in any affliction with the comfort with which we ourselves are comforted by God.

2 Corinthians 1:3-4 NASB

26

Dear Lord,

My friend is in a storm unlike any I have faced. The only way I know to help her is to tell her how faithful You are in my storms. Please calm her heart as only You can.

Amen.

"...love your enemies, do good to those
who hate you, bless those who curse you,
pray for those who mistreat you."

LUKE 6:27-28 NASB

Dear Lord,

You know how it feels to be innocent and rejected and falsely accused. You haven't told me how to pray for myself when I've been betrayed by a friend. You've only told me to love my enemies and pray for those who hurt me and mistreat me.

So Lord, I ask You to pour out Your love and all the good You want to do for the one who hurt me. And please use these prayers to heal my heart.

Amen.

As I heard the words sung, "O come, let us adore Him," it occurred to me that the first people who worshiped Jesus so genuinely at His birth adored Him when they had never seen Him do anything for them. He had not yet taught them, healed them, died for them, or redeemed them, and they adored Him. How can my own heart do less?

Dear Lord,

I don't have to know what You are going to do for me in order to adore You. I only have to know who You are. And You are everything that I need.

Amen.

"O come, let us adore Him, Christ the Lord."

FROM "O COME, ALL YE FAITHFUL" CHRISTMAS CAROL

I have been found by those who did not seek Me; I have shown (revealed) Myself to those who did not...ask for Me.

ROMANS 10:20 AMP

Dear Lord,

I don't see this one, for whose salvation I pray, seeking You at all. But Your Word says that You seek those who are not looking for You. Please seek this person and let them see their need for You.

Amen.

"For I know the plans I have for you," says the Lord. "They are plans for good and not for evil, to give you a future and a hope."

JEREMIAH 29:11 TLB

Dear Lord,

Thank You that You have a plan even though I can't see it. I bow myself to Your plan for me. I ask You to cause everything— every circumstance in my life and every enemy to Your purposes—to work with Your plan for me.

Amen.

Jesus Christ is the same yesterday and today, yes and forever.

HEBREWS 13:8 NASB

At the Metropolitan Museum of Art in New York City, I reached into my purse for my credit card, and it wasn't there. My card was signed. It said simply, "Ask for I.D." and my I.D. wasn't there either. As I dug deeper, neither was our personal checkbook or the checkbook with the funds for our business. I quickly walked the 2 ½ miles to our van to see if it all was there. What if I had lost it all? What if someone out there was having a good time with my credit card, checkbooks, and I.D.?

In the midst of my panic, it took a few minutes for me to realize that no matter what, life would go on with or without the money. No matter what happens in my life, life will go on.

Dear Lord,

Thank You that You will
always be present in my
circumstances, whatever
they may be, and that
You never change.

Amen.

We are weak, but you are [so very] strong!

1 CORINTHIANS 4:10 AMP

Therefore, He is able also to save to the uttermost...those who come to God through Him, since He is always living to make petition to God and intercede with Him and intervene for them.

HEBREWS 7:25 AMP

Dear Lord,

I'm not doing very well today, and I feel helpless to encourage myself. My faith today is nothing that would make You proud. All I know to do is to say what is true about You. I am weak, but You are strong. I am not hopeless because You sit at the right hand of the Father interceding for me. And I am not worthless because the Son of the Living God gave His life for me.

Amen.

He was before all else began and it is
his power that holds everything together.

COLOSSIANS 1:17 TLB

40

Dear Lord,

I cannot hold everything in my life together and keep it from spinning out of control. Your Word says that You have the power to hold all things together, so I'm putting it all in Your hands.

Amen.

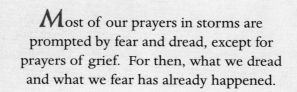

Most of our prayers in storms are prompted by fear and dread, except for prayers of grief. For then, what we dread and what we fear has already happened.

I know that there is a tomorrow when the sadness and heaviness and weariness of my heart will lift and be replaced by the sweetness of memory. But I don't know how many days away that tomorrow is.

As I wondered how to pray, I began to quote "The Lord's Prayer" and when I got to "Give us this day…" I stopped. That's what I need— to be given this day to endure the sadness.

Dear Lord,

Give me this day to endure the sadness
of my loss. Moment by moment
let me be aware of Your presence.
Day by day help me to remember
Your understanding of loss and
to consider Your great love for me.

Amen.

> *"If...My people who are called by My name*
> *humble themselves and pray, and seek My face*
> *and turn from their wicked ways, then I will*
> *hear from heaven, will forgive their sin,*
> *and will heal their land."*

2 CHRONICLES 7:14 NASB

*T*error has brought us the realization that we live
in a world where storms are always brewing,
although we may not know where. We are
supported by an economy that can be collapsed
by fear. We enjoy personal liberties that may be
surrendered for the hope of safety. Our thoughts
quickly turn to the only One who can help us.

44

Dear Lord,

As we see how our whole culture can collapse around us, and as we call and ask You to be our God, help us remember to first be Your people. You have always been God, but we have not all been Your people. Forgive us, Lord.

Amen.

45

And we know that God causes all things to work together for good to those who love God, to those who are called according to His purpose.

ROMANS 8:28 NASB

Dear Lord,

I know that You love me even though You have permitted what has happened in my life. Sometimes that love feels severe, but it is still very real love. Please give me glimpses of the sweeter showers of love that are ahead for me. Be my hope until better times come.

Amen.

Create in me a new, clean heart, O God,
filled with clean thoughts and right desires...
And when my heart is right, then you
will rejoice in the good that I do.

PSALM 51:10,19 TLB

Dear Lord,

Help me to remember not to use the situation I
face as an excuse for speaking recklessly and
reacting unkindly but rather as an opportunity
to please You with clean hands and a pure heart.

Amen.

49

We can rejoice, too, when we run into problems and trials, for we know that they are good for us—they help us learn to be patient. And patience develops strength of character in us and helps us trust God more each time we use it until finally our hope and faith are strong and steady. Then, when that happens, we are able to hold our heads high no matter what happens and know that all is well, for we know how dearly God loves us.

ROMANS 5:3-5 TLB

Dear Lord,

It seems that bad news and suffering come quickly—and leave very slowly. Patience is a fruit of Your Spirit. Please give me Your patience to endure this storm.

Amen.

51

As I watch the news, I see buildings that might be vulnerable to vehicles with explosives become fortresses. Concrete barriers are brought in and placed between that building and disaster. How I wish I could call a fortress company who could place invisible barriers around my life to keep trouble away!

Sandy Lynam Clough

*He who dwells in the secret place of the Most
High shall remain stable and fixed under the
shadow of the Almighty...I will say of the Lord,
He is my Refuge and my Fortress, my God;
on Him I lean and rely, and in Him I...trust!*

PSALM 91:1-2 AMP

Dear Lord,

Thank You, Lord, that You are a fortress for
me and that I can run to You and be sheltered.

Amen.

Above all things have intense and unfailing love for one another, for love covers a multitude of sins [forgives and disregards the offenses of other].

1 PETER 4:8 AMP

54

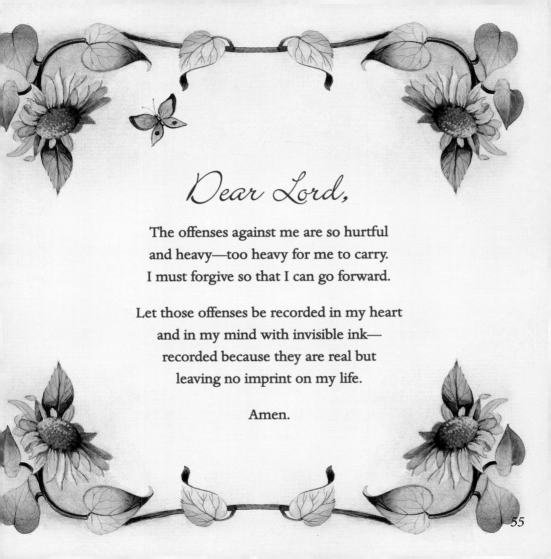

Dear Lord,

The offenses against me are so hurtful
and heavy—too heavy for me to carry.
I must forgive so that I can go forward.

Let those offenses be recorded in my heart
and in my mind with invisible ink—
recorded because they are real but
leaving no imprint on my life.

Amen.

And He arose and rebuked the wind and said to the sea, Hush now! Be still!...And the wind ceased... and there was immediately a great calm...He said to them, "Why are you so timid and fearful? How is it that you have no faith?..." And they were filled with great awe and feared exceedingly and said one to another, Who then is this, that even wind and sea obey Him?

MARK 4:39-41 AMP

Sandy Lynam Clough

Dear Lord,

You commanded the storm to be quiet. But when I try to command the things and people around me, the storm just gets worse! Help me to keep quiet and let You speak to the storm. Help me to remember to just hang on to the side of the boat and let You control the storm.

Amen.

Now glory be to God, who by his mighty power at work within us is able to do far more than we would ever dare to ask or even dream of—infinitely beyond our highest prayers, desires, thoughts, or hopes.

EPHESIANS 3:20 TLB

Dear Lord,

I have asked You to heal me many times,
but I am so convinced of Your love for me that
I cannot ask You to heal me again.   What if Your love
for me caused You to answer that prayer when You really
wanted to give me something even better than healing?
Please give me what You know is best instead
of my will and what I think is best.

Amen.

*"Therefore, everyone who hears these words of Mine
and acts upon them, may be compared to a wise man, who built
his house upon the rock. And the rain fell, and the floods came, and
the winds blew, and slammed against that house; and yet
it did not fall; for it had been founded on the rock."*

MATTHEW 7:24-25 NASB

For who is God, but the Lord?
And who is a rock, except our God.

PSALM 18:31 NASB

Dear Lord,

You are the rock that I can build my life on. You
are upright and faithful to Your promises. You are
my rock and there is no unrighteousness in You.

Amen.

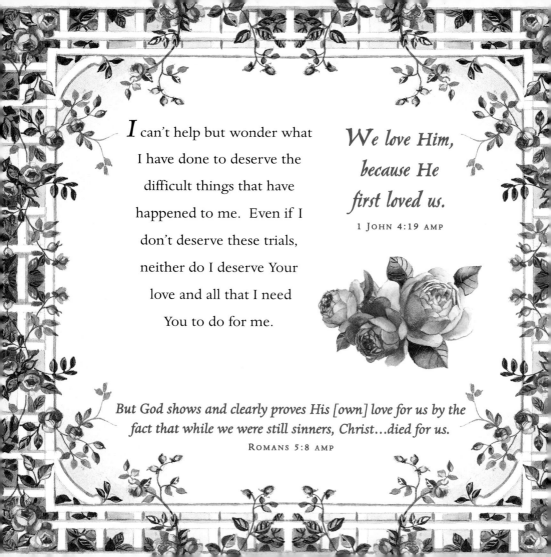

I can't help but wonder what I have done to deserve the difficult things that have happened to me. Even if I don't deserve these trials, neither do I deserve Your love and all that I need You to do for me.

We love Him, because He first loved us.

1 JOHN 4:19 AMP

But God shows and clearly proves His [own] love for us by the fact that while we were still sinners, Christ...died for us.

ROMANS 5:8 AMP

Dear Lord,

I am not worthy of Your merciful love,

but I accept Your love because I need it

so very much. Thank You for loving

me before I even knew to ask.

Amen.

Oh, give thanks to
the Lord, for He is good;
for His mercy and loving-kindness
endure forever.

1 CHRONICLES 16:34 AMP

Dear Lord,

I thank You for every storm you have kept from me,
for every car that did not hit mine, for every tornado
that missed my house, for every germ and mutant cell
that has not prospered in my body. I thank You for
every storm You kept me in and the confidence in You
it brought. And in faith, I thank You for this storm
and Your goodness towards me.

Amen.